Meeting the Challenge:

A practical approach to transition from Reception to Year 1

based on work at Albert Bradbeer Primary School, Birmingham

by Clare Shaw and Elaine Dupree

Meeting the Challenge!

ISBN 1 905019 43 2

The authors wish to record their appreciation and gratitude for the kind support of The Headteacher, Mr Colin Smith, the Governors, staff and parents of Albert Bradbeer Infant and Nursery School. They are also indebted to the wonderful children at the school, who have responded so positively to all the changes introduced.

First published in the UK, November 2005

Featherstone Education Ltd
44-46 High Street
Husbands Bosworth
Leicestershire
LE17 6LP

www.featherstone.uk.com

Contents

Introduction

Albert Bradbeer School is a two-form entry infant school in the suburbs of a large city. By September 2002 the Foundation Curriculum had been fully established in both the Nursery and Reception units.

Our emphasis had been on developing autonomy and independence through choice and play-based learning. The children had responded well to this, and by the end of reception had become used to a flexible style of working which gave them opportunities for freedom and self expression. The transition to Year 1 in that year was considered by all involved to be very difficult for some children. They found the move to a more formal environment with no opportunities to exercise any choice very hard to cope with. This resulted in challenging behaviour and some real disruption. Therefore, as September 2003 approached transition became increasingly an issue for much thought and discussion.

It was decided that, rather than change and adapt the end of the Reception year, it would be more appropriate to develop and extend the children's valuable and successful Foundation experiences into Year 1.

> *Everything we now know tells us that a 'bottom up' model, where the best of foundation practice is extended into Year 1 is more likely to be successful than over preparation of children in a 'top down' model which puts inappropriate pressure on children in Reception.*
>
> *'Smooth Transitions', Bayley and Featherstone 2003.*

The document 'Excellence and Enjoyment: a strategy for primary schools' helped us to approach the changes we were contemplating with confidence. 'The fusion of excellence and enjoyment' (ibid. p1) seemed to fit entirely with our beliefs about transition and the evolution of the curriculum in Year 1.

> *Children learn better when they are excited and engaged... When there is joy in what they are doing, they learn to love learning.*
>
> *'Excellence and Enjoyment', DfES 2003*

The problem we faced was one that every school with Key Stage 1 children faces: how to build on what children have experienced in the Foundation Stage while addressing the objectives of the National Curriculum and the Literacy and Numeracy Strategies. We had always considered children to be 'active learners' (Bayley and Featherstone 2003, p.21) and the success of our children in the Reception unit, where they had been encouraged to become autonomous and independent, supported our beliefs. It seemed to us to make no sense to suddenly transport children from one style of learning, to which they had responded well, to another which placed unwelcome and unfamiliar burdens on them.

The approach we took was designed to value and develop the skills of self-management practised by our Reception children, and to maintain motivation by encouraging autonomous choice and responsibility. We began by examining the principles set out in 'Excellence and Enjoyment' and 'Smooth Transitions', and deciding what conditions and learning experiences would contribute to these. To provide them we devised a series of 'challenges' matched to objectives in Literacy, Numeracy, Science, ICT and the Creative area. The objectives and the challenges to meet them are presented in the following pages.

Challenges are independent activities, based on the medium term planning. They are very important in encouraging the children to take responsibility for their own learning and also to make the important links between subjects. They also encourage the children to use their thinking and reasoning skills and allow them to learn in active and dynamic ways.

The children had been used to working as a unit in Reception and this had proved successful for both them and the staff. This system was continued into Year 1 and facilitated by the physical changes made to the location of the classrooms with a screen partition being added. Learning bays were created in the rooms to reflect the areas of the National Curriculum. Two teacher days were also allocated at the beginning of the school year to provide sufficient time for the reorganisation.

The challenges for the core subjects are always differentiated to ensure that the children are able to achieve success. Higher achievers are set more challenging targets, and lower achievers are set a target which they can complete independently. This then in itself fosters their self-esteem, as they are able to achieve something by themselves. Each week the children are given at least six new challenges to ensure they have a choice. All children then take responsibility for completing five challenges in their own special book. If the children complete five challenges by Friday, they are allowed to choose their own reward. The system of challenges had been introduced in Reception with the children completing one or two challenges per week in order for them to become familiar with the new system.

Teaching Literacy and Numeracy through a balance of whole class input and adult-supported small group work coupled with providing the children with weekly challenges, seemed an ideal way of supporting 'sustained shared thinking' (Bayley and Featherstone, 2003 p.17) and for accommodating different learning styles. The Senior Management team led the initiative with the full involvement of the Year 1 teaching and support staff. As this scheme was a new way of working for the school, evaluation procedures were established which included both internal and external monitoring. A new flexible timetable was established, with all Year 1 staff involved in medium and short term planning. The remaining staff were also kept informed through regular staff meetings and feedback was obtained through staff questionnaires.

Our curriculum and practices in Year 1 continue to be adapted to suit the changing needs of the children. The transition from Year 1 to Year 2 was considered in September 2004 but so far no major changes have been made and this continues to be an area of development for the school. Our changes and adaptations have hopefully made our curriculum much more child-centred than the traditional year one classroom with our focus on learning rather than on teaching. The system of challenges also motivates the children to become engaged with their learning and the flexible timetable allows us to follow up on children's interests.

The challenges for each curriculum area are outlined in the following pages. Each challenge relates to a medium term objective of the National Curriculum.

Theoretical basis and links to practice

The work described in this book reflects some of the current thinking and research into brain development and the debate concerning formal and less formal approaches to teaching and learning currently topical in education as a whole. The following table shows how our current practice and ethos in Year 1 links to documents that we have considered in coming to our decisions regarding transition from the Foundation Stage to Year 1. It also shows the development of our new systems, routines and overall philosophy. The documents referred to are:

Smooth Transitions: ensuring continuity from the Foundation Stage. Bayley and Featherstone 2003 (p.17-38, Teaching CLEVER)

Excellence and Enjoyment: a strategy for Primary Schools. DfES 2003 (p.29 The Principles of learning and teaching.)

In 'Smooth Transitions' Bayley and Featherstone introduce the concept of 'CLEVER' teaching. They describe this as 'using everything we already know and everything we are finding out about how children learn to help in our work.' (p17–38) This was what we wanted for our children, and we decided to use the definition of 'CLEVER' teaching set out in 'Smooth Transitions' as the foundation for our development work.

'CLEVER' teaching is

C – CHILD CENTRED

L – LEARNING FOCUSED

E – ENGAGING

V – VALUE–BASED

E – EFFICIENT AND EFFECTIVE

R – REALISTIC

Aim from Excellence and Enjoyment	Smooth Transitions		Practice in Year 1
Ensure every child succeeds: provide an inclusive education within a culture of high expectations.	C	Child-centered: Starting with the child, taking into account all we know about how children develop as learners.	Small group based work, particularly in Literacy and Numeracy, to ensure that children receive the maximum amount of adult support possible, allied to a system of ongoing assessment of individuals through the group books.
	L	Learning not teaching focused: Ensure that children are really getting what they need.	
	E	Effective and Efficient: A clear focus on children's learning will ensure efficient use of time, space, resources and people.	Small group work also allows work to be targeted more effectively to suit the needs of individuals. The flexibility of the timetable ensures that all children receive the maximum amount of adult support possible.
Build on what learners already know: structure and pace teaching so that students know what is to be learnt, how and why.	C	Child-centered: Starting with the child, taking into account all we know about how children develop as learners.	Small group based work, particularly in Literacy and Numeracy, to ensure that children receive the maximum amount of adult support possible, allied to a system of ongoing assessment of individuals through the group books.
	L	Learning not teaching focused: Ensure that children are really getting what they need.	
	V	Valuing children: Valuing children and their achievements.	The continuation of the group book recording system from Reception ensures that all staff are aware of the children's progress as children are supported by all staff in rotation.
Make learning vivid and real: develop understanding through enquiry, creativity, e-learning and group problem solving.	E	Engaging: To engage every child we need to engage all sorts of learners, all interests.	The mixture of small group, whole class teaching and the challenges enables a full range of experiences to be delivered. The whole ethos of praise for efforts made as well as for achievements ensures that children are confident in 'having a go', cooperation with others, negotiation and problem solving.
	V	Valuing children: Valuing children and their achievements.	

Continued on page 8

Aim from Excellence and Enjoyment	Smooth Transitions		Practice in Year 1
Make learning an enjoyable and challenging experience: stimulate learning through matching teaching techniques and strategies to a range of learning styles.	**L** **E** **V**	Learning not teaching focused: Ensure that children are really getting what they need. Engaging: To engage every child we need to engage all sorts of learners, all interests. Valuing children: Valuing children and their achievements.	The full range of learning styles can be accommodated through the flexibility of the methods used. The challenges encourage the children to make links between the areas of learning for themselves.
Enrich the learning experience: build learning skills across the curriculum.	**E** **V** **R**	Engaging: To engage every child we need to engage all sorts of learners, all interests. Valuing children: Valuing children and their achievements. Realistic: Focus on what children can do and should be doing. A focus on sustained shared thinking in the real world.	The challenges encourage the children to make links between the areas of learning for themselves. This can then be followed up individually and in whole group situations.
Promote assessment for learning: make children partners in their learning.	**C** **V** **E** **R**	Child-centered: Starting with the child, taking into account all we know about how children develop as learners. Valuing children: Valuing children and their achievements. Effective and Efficient: A clear focus on children's learning will ensure efficient use of time, space, resources and people. Realistic: Focus on what children can do and should be doing. A focus on sustained shared thinking in the real world.	Small group based work, particularly in Literacy and Numeracy, to ensure that children receive maximum adult support, allied to a system of ongoing assessment of individuals through the group books. The ethos of team working, and the whole year group as one unit means that staff, time, and resources can be used to best effect. Staff are able to fill a variety of roles, share planning and assessments of the children, and share the making and preparation of resources.

Aims of the initiative

- To ensure a successful transition for the children moving from Reception to Year 1, so that children's emotional well-being, self-esteem and sense of security remain high throughout the process.

- To establish a learning environment in Year 1, which extends and develops the successful experiences of the Foundation Curriculum, so that children's abilities to think, reason and to learn in active and dynamic ways are fostered and developed.

Introduction to the challenge system

Challenges are independent activities that are based on the medium term planning covering all areas of the curriculum.

Each week the children are given six new challenges to ensure they have a choice. All children then take responsibility for completing five challenges in their own special book. If the children complete five challenges by Friday, they are allowed to choose their own reward from a menu of options. Children who complete a really good challenge receive a challenge champ badge and their work is displayed in the 'Fantastic Challenge Work' folder.

In order to ensure that every child has access to help we have introduced the role of 'challenge support'. In each session three adults work directly with small groups. A fourth adult is focused on supporting children with their challenges by:

$\sum$ • extending the thinking and reasoning skills of the more able.

$\sum$ • ensuring the quality of work reflects each child's individual ability.

$\sum$ • providing individual support or alternative strategies for the less able, e.g. by encouraging mixed ability, peer support buddies.

$\sum$ • checking and signing off completed challenges.

Our approach to the teaching of Literacy and Numeracy through a balance of whole class input and adult supported small group work relies on a record book where ongoing formative assessments and observations can be recorded. There is a record book for each of the ability groups. This enables all staff to monitor and pass on individual attainment and learning needs.

The combination of small group work and weekly challenges seemed to us the most effective way of supporting 'sustained shared thinking' (Bayley and Featherstone 2003, p.17) and of making the learning appropriate to the child by accommodating different learning styles.

How to use this book

The challenges we have devised for Literacy and Numeracy, which are detailed on the following pages, are directly related to the half-termly objectives outlined in the strategies. The intention throughout the development of the challenges has been to foster cross-curricular links and creativity. The result is that wherever possible subjects include the development of skills in other areas. Therefore, the book is arranged into half termly sections that include the challenges for all areas of the curriculum based on the QCA topics. This enables readers to select the parts most appropriate for their own setting. Some of the challenges we use in school require specific resources. We have not included these and have concentrated on activities which can be adapted to suit the resources that are liekly to be available in most settings.

The topics arranged as follows:

Autumn 1	Science – Ourselves	Geography – Our Local Area
Autumn 2	Science – Light and Dark	Geography – Our Local Area
Spring 1	Science – Materials	History – Toys from the Past
Spring 2	Science – Forces	Geography – Comparing our area with another locality
Summer 1	Science – Growth	History - Homes from the past
Summer 2	Science – Sound and Hearing	As there is no set History or Geography topic in this half term, the children are encouraged to devise their own challenges. Each ability group constructs its own challenge with the help of an adult to ensure that high expectations are maintained.

The last section of the book, 'Challenges in action', combines photographs with comments by parents, staff and children to provide different perspectives on how challenges work in our setting.

We realise that all settings are different but we hope that this account of our work will provide some food for thought.

The following pages list the curriculum objectives and the challenges we have devised to meet them. We try to cater for the different learning needs and abilities of our children by setting many of the challenges at several levels - for higher, medium and lower achievers. Sometimes even these are adapted for individuals by the teacher in the light of her knowledge of a particular child. When no ability level is indicated the challenge is the same for all children. We often put children of mixed abilities together for stimulation and support.

Many of the challenges rely on our own resources and methods of working. We do not use them ourselves as a scheme of work, and they are not presented here as that. We hope rather that readers will use them to trigger ideas and provoke their own thinking, adapting our approach, challenges and methods to their own settings.

Literacy Challenges Autumn 1

Objectives from NLS	Challenges
Use full stops, capital letters and finger spaces appropriately.	Draw a picture of your friend and write a sentence to describe what makes them special.
Write about events in personal experience linked to a variety of familiar incidents form stories.	Write a letter to a character in a book, make an envelope and address it. *We stipulate a character from the child's own reading book in our reading scheme (The Oxford Reading Tree).*
Practice and secure the ability to hear initial and final phonemes in cvc words.	Write the appropriate letter sounds by each picture.
Write a simple sentences and to re-read recognising whether or not they make sense.	Write a sentence about yourself using 'I am' or 'I can'.
Practice and secure the ability to hear initial and final phonemes in cvc words. (Reception link)	Draw a picture and write at least an initial letter for each thing you have drawn.
Write captions for their own work.	Draw a picture of a scary character from a story (e.g. the wolf from Little Red Riding Hood) and label the nasty features e.g. straggly hair, big nose, claws.
Use of the grammar of a sentence to predict new or unfamiliar words. Practice and secure the ability to hear initial sounds in cvc words.	Higher and Middle achievers: complete the missing words about Handa's Surprise. *We use a worksheet which gives a simple retelling of the story with selected key words left out.* Lower achievers: draw 3 or 4 of the fruits in Handa's Surprise and write the initial sound for each.
Write captions for their own work.	Draw a picture of an owl and use interesting adjectives to describe it.
Make simple lists for planning, reminding etc.	Write a list of interesting party food, e.g. crunchy carrots.
Practice and secure alphabetic letter knowledge and order. (Reception link)	Higher and Middle achievers: using letters A-L, draw and label the given pictures in alphabetical order. Lower achievers: using letters A-D, draw and label the given pictures in alphabetical order. *We have a selection of cut out pictures. The children arrange them in alphabetical order, then copy them and label their drawings.*

Literacy Challenges Autumn 2

Objectives from NLS	Challenges
Begin to use full stops to demarcate sentences and to use a capital letter for the personal pronoun 'I'.	Higher achievers: write 2 or 3 sentences about what you did in the holiday. Lower achievers: write a sentence about what you did in the holiday.
Read and use captions, e.g. labels around school on equipment.	Write a label/caption for something around school.
Write captions for their own work.	Label a vehicle or piece of equipment that would be used by one of the people who help us.
Write and draw simple instructions. (Reception link to Foundation Stage re. sequencing)	Higher and Middle achievers: write some instructions for making a tasty sandwich. Lower achievers: put the pictures showing the little girl getting ready for school in order. *We have a sequence of cut out pictures which we give to the children in random order.*
Re-enact stories in a variety of ways eg through role play using dolls or puppets.	Use puppets to re-tell the story of the Wizard of Oz.
Make simple lists for planning.	Write a Christmas list for Santa.
Know new words from reading and shared experiences and to make collections of personal interest or significant words and words linked to particular topics.	Complete the Christmas word search. *We have several Christmas word searches at different levels of difficulty. We choose the one most suitable for the child.*

Literacy Challenges Spring 1

Objectives from NLS	Challenges
Secure identification, spelling and reading of initial, final and medial letter sounds in simple words.	Higher achievers: write as many words as you can which rhyme with the four given words. Middle achievers: as above with 3 words. Lower achievers: as above 3 words.
Know new words from reading and shared experiences and to make collections of personal interest or significant words and words linked to particular topics.	Higher achievers: write 3/4 sentences using the given word bank. *The word bank is based on words from the big book of the week or on a cross-curricular theme related to a topic in science or history.* Middle achievers: as above but 2/3 sentences. Lower achievers: write the initial sound by the picture of a character from this week's story.
Build simple profiles of characters from stories read.	Higher achievers: draw a horrible monster and a nice monster. Describe them, using adjectives. Middle and Higher achievers: draw and write 2 sentences about a horrible monster. Lower achievers: draw and write 1 sentence about a horrible monster.
Write captions for their own work.	Higher achievers: choose 3 toys from the class museum and write a label for each, using adjectives. *We set up a class museum with the children to link with our History topic for this half term 'Toys from the Past'. We involved the children in organising the toys and making signs and labels for the museum.* Middle achievers: choose 2 toys from the class museum and write a label for each. Lower achievers; choose 1 toy from the class museum and write a label for it.

continues over

Literacy Challenges Spring 1 (continued)

Objectives from NLS	Challenges
Become aware of character and dialogue.	Higher achievers: make a speech and thought bubble for Preston and the wolf. *This challenge was linked to our big book of the week 'Suddenly' by Colin McNaughton but would work as successfully for any character from any story.* Middle and Lower achievers: make either a speech or thought bubble for the above characters.
Use simple sentences to describe pictures based on their own experience.	Higher achievers: use interesting adjectives to describe 5 given pictures in sentences. *The pictures could be of anything that the children can relate to or are familiar with. However, children love looking at pictures of themselves working or playing in the classroom so we used these. They were subsequently very motivated to write a sentence to match the photographs.* Middle and Lower achievers: write a simple sentence to describe each of 3 given pictures.

Literacy Challenges Spring 2

Objectives from NLS	Challenges
Use simple dictionaries and to understand their alphabetical organisation.	Higher achievers: work in pairs to make your own dictionary of minibeasts/animals. Try to use all the letters from A to Z. Middle and Lower achievers: as above but to at least J.
Use simple dictionaries and to understand their alphabetical organisation.	Higher achievers: use a dictionary to help you find out the meaning of 5 given words. *The words are taken either from the NLS keyword lists or specific vocabulary related to our Science or Geography topics.* Middle and Lower achievers: as above but 3 given familiar words.
Assemble information from your own experience and to use simple sentences to describe them.	Higher achievers: Draw a picture of where you live. Write about it. Middle and Lower achievers: Draw a picture of where you live and write 1 sentence about it.
Write simple non-chronological reports.	Higher achievers: draw a map of your journey home and describe it. Middle achievers: draw 3 things that you pass on the way home and describe them. Lower achievers: draw and label 3 things you pass on your journey home.
Produce extended captions.	Higher achievers: make a poster to describe a pet you would like. Write at least 5 sentences, using lots of adjectives. Middle achievers: as above but write 3 sentences. Lower achievers: as above but fewer sentences.

Literacy Challenges Summer 1

Objectives from NLS	Challenges
Write simple recounts linked to personal experience.	Higher achievers: write 5 interesting sentences about what you did in the holidays. Middle and Lower achievers: write 3 interesting sentences about what you did in the holidays.
Write about significant incidents from known stories.	Higher achievers: invent an alien. Draw a picture of it and describe it, saying what it's like and where it lives. Use lots of adjectives in your description. Middle and Lower achievers: invent an alien. Draw and label a picture of it.
Use poems or parts of poems as models for their own writing eg by substituting words.	Higher achievers: choose one of the given incomplete poems. Add your own rhymes to finish each line. *Simple rhyming poems were selected from an anthology.* Middle and Lower achievers: complete 'Twinkle, Twinkle Little Star'.
Compose own poetic sentences using repetitive patterns.	Higher achievers: work in pairs to write your own rhyming poem. Middle and Lower achievers: write 2 rhyming sentences.
Write simple recounts linked to topics of interest.	Higher achievers: write a sentence describing how each room in a Victorian house differs from their own house. *This challenge relates to the History topic for this half term, 'Homes from the past'.* Middle achievers: write a sentence describing how the kitchen and bathroom in a Victorian house differs from their own house. Lower achievers: write a sentence describing how the kitchen in a Victorian house differs from their own house.
Recognise new words from reading and shared experiences, and to make collections of significant words linked to a particular topic.	Higher achievers: complete the jungle word search and put 2 words from the search into a sentence. Think about how you can make the sentence really interesting. *The word search was based on the animals from the book 'Rumble in the Jungle' which the children had enjoyed the previous week.* Middle and Lower achievers: complete the jungle word search and put 1 word from the search into a sentence.

Literacy Challenges Summer 2

Objectives from NLS	Challenges
Expect reading to make sense and check if it does not. Recognise words by common spelling patterns.	Higher achievers: complete cloze procedure and match 7 capital letters to their lower case letter. *The cloze procedure exercises were differentiated according the words that the children had to use. These were all based on the NLS keyword lists.* Middle achievers: complete cloze procedure and match 5 capital letters to their lower case letter. Lower abilities: look at the pictures and write some rhyming words
Continue demarcating sentences in writing ending a sentence with a full stop.	Higher achievers: look at given sentences and rewrite them, using capital letters and full stops. Middle and Lower achievers: look at 3 given sentences and rewrite them, using capital letters and full stops.
Write simple recounts linked to topics of interest.	Higher achievers: write 8 sentences describing what you would choose to be if you could become something else for a day (e.g. an animal, a monster). What would you look like? What would you do? How would you behave? Middle and Lower achievers: as above but 4 sentences.
Write for a given purpose and communicate ideas to peers.	Higher achievers: write a list of 5 challenges that you would like to do next week. Middle and Lower achievers: as above but 3 challenges.

Numeracy Challenges Autumn 1

Objectives from NLS	Challenges
Read and write numerals to at least 10.	Start at 1 and write all the numbers that you can.
Order numbers to 10 (extension to 20) and position them on a number line.	Higher achievers: order the digit cards 0-20. Middle and Lower achievers: order the digit cards 0-10.
Recognise simple repeating patterns and use 1 or more shapes to make a repeating pattern.	Use the given 2D shapes to make a repeating pattern.
Understand the operation of addition and use the related vocab. (Begin to use the appropriate signs to record a number sentence)	Higher achievers: use the ladybird outline and mark 10 spots on the 2 wings of the ladybird. Record the sum in your book. *The children were given the option of either drawing their own ladybird or using some large A4 size, simple ladybird outlines which were made available.* Middle and Lower achievers: arrange 5 spots on the 2 wings of the ladybird. Draw in your book.
Understand the operation of subtraction and use the related vocab.	Higher achievers: Handa's subtraction sheet to 15. *This challenge related to our big book of the week 'Handa's Surprise'. The subtraction sheet contained differentiated questions (1-10 lower, 11 & 12 middle and 13-15 higher), and had pictures of the fruit to help the children with their subtraction sums. We also made some fruit shaped counters which the children tcould use to work out the answers practically.* Middle achievers: as above to 12. Lower achievers: as above to 10.

Numeracy Challenges Autumn 1 (continued)

Objectives from NLS	Challenges
Solve simple money problems set in a real life context. Recognise and begin to use 1p, 2p (and 5p) coins.	Higher achievers: choose an object that costs between 10p and 15p. Use 1p, 2p and 5p pieces to pay for it. Middle achievers: as above but buying objects to 10p. Lower achievers: as middle achievers but using only 1p pieces.
Understand the operation of addition and subtraction and use the related vocab.	Higher achievers: solve the given addition and subtraction sums to 20. *The children were given a selection of differentiated sums. They then had to pick a specific number themselves and copy and complete them into their books.* Middle achievers: as above but to 15. Lower achievers: as above but to 12.

Numeracy Challenges Autumn 2

Objectives from NLS	Challenges
Read and write numerals to at least 10.	Higher achievers: write all your numbers to 20, thinking about the correct formation. Middle achievers: as above but to 15. Lower achievers: as above but to 10.
Describe and extend number sequences.	Higher achievers: complete number patterns counting in 2s to 30. Middle achievers: as above but to 20. Lower achievers: write the numeral next to the appropriate number of objects.
Read and write numerals in words.	Higher achievers: match numerals to words (numbers 5 – 20) Middle achievers: as above but using numbers to 10. Lower achievers: as above but using numbers to 5.
Solve mathematical problems (write as many different ways as you can of making the number 9)	Higher achievers: make 5 addition or subtraction sums that have 9 as the answer. Middle achievers: find the addition and subtraction sums that have 9 as the answer. Lower achievers: find the addition sums that have 9 as the answer.
Read time on a clock to 1 hour and half an hour	Higher achievers: use the clock stamp to print 3 clocks and put a time on them (using o'clock and half past). Draw a picture of what you would be doing at each time. Middle achievers: as above but only 2 clocks. Lower achievers: as above but only using o'clock.

Numeracy Challenges Spring 1

Objectives from NLS	Challenges
Use everyday language to describe features of familiar 2D shapes.	Draw and cut out some 2D shapes to make your own 'shape' picture.
Understand the operation of subtraction and the related vocabulary.	Higher and middle achievers: pick a subtraction sum to 30, and copy and solve it in your book. Lower achievers: solve the pictorial subtraction problems to 12.
Recall all pairs of numbers which total 10 (20 and 5).	Higher achievers: in your own way, write all the number bonds to 10 and 20. Middle achievers: as above but to 10. Lower achievers: as above but to 5.
Measure mass using non-standard units. Compare 2 masses using direct comparison.	Higher achievers: use simple balances to weigh 2 objects using cubes. Draw in your book the object and the number of cubes. Ring which was the heavier object. Middle and Lower achievers: as above but weigh only 1 object.
Recognise coins of different value and find totals.	Higher achievers: choose a picture of an object priced up to 25p and draw the coins you could use to buy it. Middle achievers: as above but to 15p. Lower achievers: as above but to 10p.
Solve simple problems involving money and explain how the problem was solved.	Higher achievers: choose 2 purses and total the coins (up to 25p). Middle achievers: as above but to 15p Lower achievers: as above but to 10p.

Numeracy Challenges Spring 2

Objectives from NLS	Challenges
Continue to recognise all even numbers to 20.	Higher achievers: write all numbers to 30 on the given grid and colour in all even numbers green. What do you notice? Middle achievers: as above but to 20. Lower achievers: as above to 15.
Solve mathematical problems or puzzles.	Higher achievers: what sums can you make which have 24 as the answer? Middle achievers: as above but with 10 as the answer. Lower achievers: as above but with 5 as the answer.
Begin to recognise that 2 or more numbers can be added together.	Higher achievers: use 3 numbers to make sums with the answer as 15. Middle achievers: solve the addition sums to 20. Lower achievers: solve the addition sums to 15.
Suggest and use suitable non-standard/standard units and measuring equipment to compare 2 different lengths.	Higher achievers: use a ruler to measure the length of the dinosaurs. Write which one is the longest and which is the shortest. *We traced pictures to make some paper cut-out dinosaurs, which the children can then measure using a ruler.* Middle and Lower achievers: use cubes to measure the lengths of the dinosaurs and put a tick by the longest dinosaur.
Solve simple problems involving length.	Higher achievers: use a ruler to measure the length of 5 different given items. *A variety of objects are made available to the children, from around 3cm to 20cm in length.* Middle and Lower achievers: as above but 3 items.
Understand and use the vocabulary related to length.	Higher achievers: measure and record the length of the 5 snakes using string and a ruler. *We use a variety of plastic snakes from a toy shop.* Middle and Lower achievers: as above but 3 items.

Numeracy Challenges Summer 1

Objectives from NLS	Challenges
Know by heart all pairs of numbers which total 10 (ext 20).	Higher achievers: write all the number bonds to 20. Middle and Lower achievers: write all the number bonds to 10.
Recognise the use of symbols to stand for an unknown number.	Higher achievers: copy and complete the rocket addition and subtraction sums into your book. *The sums are presented in the shape of a rocket. This links with our Literacy big book about space and aliens.* Middle achievers: as above but the addition sums only. Lower achievers: write the numbers to 12 in the correct order and complete the 3 rocket addition sums.
Begin to use the vocabulary of ordinal numbers.	Higher achievers: play a race game using ordinal numbers and five cars. *The children play the game in groups of five, using toy cars and a race board. They use ordinal numbers to record the finishing order of the cars.* Middle and Lower achievers: as above but 3 cars.
Use 2D shapes to make/describe repeating patterns.	Higher achievers: make repeating patterns using 4 colours and 4 shapes. Middle and Lower achievers: as above using 2/3 colours and shapes.
Say a number that is 1/10 more/less than a given number.	Higher achievers: choose a digit card (20–50) and write a number that is 10 more and one that is 10 less. Middle achievers: as above but using numbers to 20 and 1 more/less. Lower achievers: as middle but using numbers to 15.
Begin to understand symmetry and make symmetry patterns.	Higher achievers: make your own symmetrical picture using the given grid. *The children are given a piece of A4, squared paper. They then draw their own line of symmetry and use this to create a symmetrical picture or pattern.* Middle and Lower achievers: complete the other half of the given picture.

Numeracy Challenges Summer 2

Objectives from NLS	Challenges
Recognise and extend number sequences with differences of 1, 2 and 5.	Higher achievers: complete and extend the number sequences to 50 in steps of 2s and 5s. Middle achievers: complete and extend the number sequences to 26 in steps of 2. Lower achievers: complete and extend the number sequences to 15 in steps of 1.
Read time on a clock to 1 hour and half an hour.	Higher achievers: print 5 clocks and put the time on them (using o'clock and half past). Middle achievers: as above but only 3 clocks. Lower achievers: as above but only 2 clocks and using only an hour hand.
Know what each digit in a number represents and partition a number into a multiple of 10's and 1's.	Higher achievers: pick 5 numbers to 100 and partition them into tens and units. Tell your partner another number that has either the same number of tens or the same number of units as each of your 5 numbers. *eg if the child had picked 34 initially, another number with the same number of tens could be 36; or one with the same number of units would be 54.* Middle achievers: as above but 5 numbers to 50. Lower achievers: pick 3 numbers to 25 and tell your partner how many tens and units
Solve simple problems involving money: find totals and give change.	Higher achievers: pick 2 items from the class shop. Pay with a 10p, 20p or 50p and work out how much change the shopkeeper needs to give you. Middle achievers: as above put paying with 5p, 10p or 20p. Lower achievers: buy an item from the shop and use 2p and 5p coins to pay for it.
Understand and use the vocabulary related to capacity by using uniform non-standard/standard units.	Higher achievers: find out which of 3 given containers holds the most. *These are non-standard containers. The children have to first fill each container with water and then measure this quantity in a measuring jug to determine the capacity of the container in ml.* Middle achievers: as above but 2 containers. Lower achievers: which of the two containers is half empty/full?

Science Challenges Autumn 1

Objectives linked to the QCA scheme of work: Ourselves	Challenges
Use appropriate instruments to make detailed observations.	Look at one part of your body using a magnifying glass. Tell an adult what you have found out.
Understand that humans have bodies with similar parts.	Draw and label as many parts of the body as you can.
Know that the sense of touch helps us to find out about the world.	Higher and Middle achievers: choose several items from the feely box. Draw your hand and write inside the names of 2 things that you like to touch and 2 things that you don't like to touch. *A feely box is a box which the children cannot see into but are able to put their hands inside. It is big enough to put a variety of different objects inside which they have to investigate through touch.* Lower achievers: as above but draw pictures of the items.
Know that the sense of taste helps us to find out about foods we like/dislike.	Higher and Middle achievers: draw a smiley face and a sad face and write under the smiley face a list of things that you like to eat, and under the sad face write 2 things that you don't like to eat. Lower achievers: as above but draw pictures.
Know that the sense of hearing helps us to find out about the world.	Draw a picture that shows one sound that you may hear on the way to school and one that you would hear in school.
Know that the sense of smell helps us to find out about the world.	Higher and Middle achievers: draw a smiley face and a sad face and write a list of things that you like the smell of and 2 things that you don't like to smell. Lower achievers: as above but draw pictures.
Know that we have five senses which allow us to find out about the world.	Draw a picture of yourself and label the parts of your body used for each of your senses.

Science Challenges Autumn 2

Objectives linked to the QCA scheme of work: Light and Dark	Challenges
Know that there are many sources of light.	Higher and Middle achievers: draw 3 things that give off light and label them. Lower achievers: draw 3 things that give off light.
Know that the sun is an important source of light for the earth.	Higher and Middle achievers: draw and label 2 artificial and 2 natural sources of light. Lower achievers: draw 1 natural and 1 artificial source of light.
Understand that shadows are caused by an absence of light.	Investigate what happens to the teddy's shadow when you shine the torch into the box. Draw what you see. *This activity needs to be set up by an adult. A small compare bear is put into a box which has two holes on one side. One hole is used for the child to look through and the other is big enough to shine light from a torch into the box. The children can then see how the teddy's shadow grows and shrinks as the torch is moved.*
Make comparisons between light sources.	Higher and Middle achievers: describe when you might use a torch and when you might use an electric light as sources of light. Lower achievers: draw when you might use a torch and when you might use an electric light as sources of light.
Know that light sources may vary in brightness.	Draw a picture of a place where bright lights are needed (e.g. a cave, a dungeon).
Know that some sources of light show up best at night-time.	Higher and Middle achievers: draw and label a coat that would help to keep you safe in the dark. Lower achievers: as above but just draw.
Understand that light travels through some materials better that other.	Make a pair of curtains for a bear to block out the light at night.

Science Challenges Spring 1

Objectives linked to the QCA scheme of work: Materials	Challenges
Sort objects according to their material.	Higher and Middle achievers: draw an object that is made of at least 2 different materials and label the materials. Lower achievers: draw an object and label which materials it is made of.
Group materials together and make a recording of grouping.	Higher and Middle achievers: collect 6 different materials and sort them into opaque and transparent. Lower achievers: as above but 4 materials.
Understand that every material has many properties that can be identified by using our senses.	Higher and Middle achievers: choose from the junk box 2 items that you think have things in common and 2 that are different. Draw the items and describe the similarities and differences. Lower achievers: pick 2 junk items that you think have things in common. Draw the items and describe what is similar about them.
Understand that materials are chosen for specific purposes on the basis of their properties.	Draw a picture of a house and label the different materials used to build it.
Understand that materials are chosen for specific purposes on the basis of their properties.	Draw a picture of a car. Label and describe the different materials used to make it.
Understand that some materials are attracted to a magnet.	Higher and Middle achievers: draw 2 objects that are attracted to a magnet and 2 that are not. Can you identify the material that is attracted to the magnet? Lower achievers: as above but just 1 object.

Science Challenges Spring 2

Objectives linked to the QCA scheme of work: Forces	Challenges
Recognise the movement of a range of toys.	Higher and Middle achievers: draw a picture of an object that we push or pull. Write a sentence about how the object is moved. Lower achievers: as above but just draw.
Show awareness of friction being a force. Recognise that a force can make things go faster or slower.	Higher and Middle achievers: push a model car over 3 different surfaces and record how far the car travels. Which material did the car travel the furthest over? Why? Lower achievers: as above but discuss your findings with an adult.
Understand the concept of different movements and describe using appropriate vocabulary.	Higher and Middle achievers: identify all the push/pull forces in the picture and write three sentences about the different forces. *The children are given a picture showing different forces being used, e.g. a girl pulling a dog's lead, a person pushing a pram. They are asked to identify which force is being used in each picture; i.e. a 'push' or a 'pull' force.* Lower achievers: as above but write one sentence about one of the different forces.
Understand that wind is a force. Demonstrate their understanding of forces to make their fish move.	Higher and Middle achievers: investigate different ways of making paper fish move across a paper 'pond' without touching them. Write in books which way was best and why. *For this experiment the children could decide to move the fish by making a wind force in different ways, i.e. blowing, hitting a newspaper near the fish, balloon pumps, etc.* Lower achievers: as above but discuss what happened with an adult.
Understand that water is a force.	Higher and Middle achievers: investigate floating and sinking. Make a list of objects which float and another of objects which sink. Discuss with your friend what you have found out. Lower achievers: draw 3 things that float and 3 things that sink.

Science Challenges Summer 1

Objectives linked to the QCA scheme of work: Growth	Challenges
Recognise that there are different plants in the immediate environment.	Higher and Middle achievers: draw and describe any signs of spring that you have noticed over the holidays. Lower achievers: as above but discuss observations with an adult.
Identify parts of a tree/plant using correct vocabulary.	Draw and label one of the trees/plants we observed in a science lesson, using the correct terms.
Be aware that there is a cycle of growth for all plants and trees.	Higher and Middle achievers: draw the life cycle of a sunflower and describe it. Lower achievers: as above but discuss with an adult.
Be aware that plants grow and use drawings to record observations of plant growth.	Look at the bean you have planted and record any changes that you can see. Talk about these with a friend. *As part of a Science topic, children plant a bean. This challenge encourages children to investigate any changes that have occurred to their bean.* Continue and complete your bean diary. Compare the growth of the bean you planted with the one your friend planted.
Observe and understand the role of the stem in a plant.	Higher and Middle achievers: draw and describe what happens to celery when you leave it in coloured water. *This experiment is also set up in a Science lesson, to show how water is drawn up through a plant from the roots to the leaves. The celery is put in a jam jar of coloured water to show how the leaves will eventually turn the same colour as the water.* Lower achievers: as above but draw.
Understand that plants will grow towards the light.	Higher and Middle achievers: look at the plant we put in the dark box. Draw and describe what has happened to the plant. *A peephole experiment is set up to show how plants always grow towards the light. A shoot is put in a dark box with only a small hole in one side of the box. Over time the children are able to see how the shoot grows towards the only light it can find, i.e. the hole.* Lower achievers: as above but only draw.

Science Challenges Summer 2

Objectives linked to the QCA scheme of work: Sound and Hearing	Challenges
Identify the 5 senses.	Higher and Middle achievers: identify and describe the 5 senses. Lower achievers: identify and describe at least 3 of the senses.
Make observations of sounds by listening very carefully.	Listen to the tape of school sounds. Make a picture record of the sounds you hear. *We made a tape of a selection of sounds around the school that the children would be familiar with, e.g. children talking, a bell ringing, someone playing the piano, etc.*
Know that there are many ways of describing sounds using appropriate vocabulary.	Look at the 'sound pictures' and decide how to sort them into 2 groups, e.g. outside/inside sounds or loud/soft sounds, etc. *We use a variety of pictures showing different things which make sounds, e.g. a siren on a fire engine, a bird singing, a teacher blowing a whistle, etc.*
Identify different ways that instruments make sounds.	Higher and Middle achievers: choose 5 instruments and describe their sounds using a 'sound' word. Lower achievers: as above but 3 instruments.
Understand that sound is a vibration in the air. Explore sound using other senses.	Put a balloon next to a speaker and describe what happens and what you feel. Record your findings and talk about which senses you have used.

ICT Challenges Autumn 1

Many of the ICT challenges are based on the software Tizzy's Tools. This is a programme incorporating seven tools, including a word processing, paint and turtle graphics application and chart and graph-maker programmes.

Objectives linked to the QCA scheme of work	Challenges
Know that ICT can be used to assemble and present text in different ways.	Use a writing programme to write your name. Change the colour and size of the font. *The writing programme we use is found in Tizzy's Tools.*
Produce text showing an awareness of the space bar.	Use a writing programme to write an interesting sentence about yourself. Remember to start with a capital letter and end with a full stop. *The writing programme we use is found in Tizzy's Tools.*
Use a mouse to select and move items on the screen.	Click and drag the body parts to make a person. *This is a game which can be found on the Birmingham Grid for Learning (in primary science activities) where the children have to click and drag the body parts to label a person.*
Know that text can be selected from a word bank.	Higher and Middle achievers: use the reading scheme word bank to make 2 sentences. Lower achievers: as above but only 1 sentence. *The word bank is made up of key words from the Oxford Reading Tree scheme.*
Share their ideas, presenting them in different forms.	Use a drawing programme to draw a picture of yourself or your friend using thick and thin lines. *The drawing programme we use is found in Tizzy's Tools.*
Share their ideas, presenting them in different forms. Use a text box to insert writing.	Higher and Middle achievers: use a drawing programme to draw a fruit or animal from Handa's Surprise. Label what you have drawn using the text key. Lower achievers: as above but just draw the picture. *The drawing programme we use is found in Tizzy's Tools.*

ICT Challenges Autumn 2

Objectives linked to the QCA scheme of work	Challenges
Develop skills in using a programmable computer programme.	Higher and Middle achievers: use the 'Move' programme to direct an animal from the start to his home. Change the background to one which you like. Lower achievers: as above but only direct the animal. *The turtle graphic programme we use is found on Tizzy's Tools.*
Add data onto a computer. Present their findings in a variety of ways.	Use the class data you have collected to make a bar graph of favourite playground items. Working with a partner, ask 10 friends who their favourite cartoon character is and enter this onto a bar graph. (children paired in mixed ability group) Use the class data you have collected to make a pictogram on favourite pets. *The data is collected during a whole class session and recorded (as a tally and a total) onto a large sheet of paper which the children can then refer to.*
Develop skills in using the programmable toy.	Use a programmable toy to visit the 'people who help us' on the grid. *This challenge is linked to a Geography topic about 'Our Local Area and People'. A grid was drawn on a large piece of card. We stuck pictures on the grid of, for example, a fireman, a lollipop lady, a policeman, etc. The challenge for the children was to work out how to send the pixie to a specific person.*
Share their ideas, presenting them in different forms.	Use a drawing programme to draw a firework. Higher and Middle achievers: use a drawing programme to draw a picture for your Christmas card or calendar. *We use the drawing programme in Tizzy's Tools.*
Know that ICT can be used to assemble and present text in different ways. Show awareness of the internet for communication.	E-mail santa to tell him your Christmas list.

ICT Challenges Spring 1

Objectives linked to the QCA scheme of work	Challenges
Share their ideas, presenting them in different forms.	Use a drawing programme to draw a Christmas present you would like to get, or one you would like to give to someone else. *We use the drawing programme in Tizzy's Tools.*
Use a word bank to order text on the screen.	Higher and Middle achievers: use the word bank for this term's topic to make two sentences. Lower achievers: as above but only 1 sentence.
Use a writing programme effectively to write a sentence.	Higher and Middle achievers: use a writing programme to write a sentence describing yourself. Ask a friend to change one of your words or add another adjective to make your sentence more interesting. Lower achievers: use a writing programme to write a sentence about yourself. *We use the writing programme in Tizzy's Tools.*
Use a drawing programme to share their ideas, presenting them in different forms.	Use a drawing programme to draw a character from our big book. *We use the drawing programme in Tizzy's Tools.*
Know how to save and retrieve work.	Retrieve saved work from the writing programme. Add your name and resave the file.
Use a word processing package to make alterations to text on the screen.	Higher and Middle achievers: read the given sentence and correct the 4 mistakes. Lower achievers: read the given sentence and correct the 2 mistakes. *An adult writes a sentence incorrectly, using key words from the NLS, which the children then have to correct. The adult can vary the difficulty according to the needs of the child. Again, we use Tizzy's Tools for this.*

ICT Challenges Spring 2

Objectives linked to the QCA scheme of work	Challenges
Use a word bank to order text on the screen.	Higher and Middle achievers: use our reading scheme word bank to make 2 sentences. Add some interesting adjectives to make your sentence more fun to read. Lower achievers – as above but only 1 sentence. *The word bank is made up of key words from the school reading scheme – The Oxford Reading Tree. The children then had to add their own adjectives to make the sentence more interesting.*
Use a writing programme effectively to write a sentence.	Using the given word bank, put the fruit and animals in alphabetical order. (mixed ability pairs) *The word bank is made up of familiar fruit and animals, which the children then have to click on in the correct order to produce an alphabetical list.*
Amend text using the backspace and delete key.	Higher and Middle achievers: use the backspace/delete key to correct the muddled alphabet. Lower achievers – as above but only do the first 10 letters. *A muddled alphabet was saved onto the computer by an adult for the children to rewrite in alphabetical order below.*
Highlight text in order to change the size and colour.	Write both your first name and your family name on a writing programme and change the colour and size of the text by highlighting it.
Use a drawing programme to draw a picture and use 2 different techniques for adding colour.	Use a drawing programme to draw a picture of your pet (or one you would like to have). Add colour using different techniques.
Use a drawing programme to draw a picture.	Use a drawing programme to draw a house from another country.

ICT Challenges Summer 1

Objectives linked to the QCA scheme of work	Challenges
To use a drawing programme to draw a picture.	Use a drawing programme to draw a picture of a flower. Label it. Discuss how you could improve your picture if you did it again.
To use a writing programme effectively to write a sentence.	Write an interesting sentence about your favourite challenge. Read it through with a friend to check that it makes sense. Remember to use finger spaces, capital letters and full stops.
To use an interactive web site effectively.	Higher achievers: in pairs, explore the castle on the interactive site and write an account of how life in a castle would have been different from life in a house today. Middle and Lower achievers: as above but discuss the site with a grown up. *Website address: http://kotn.ntu.ac.yk/castle/view.html*
To amend retrieved work and resave it.	Retrieve saved work from the writing programme. Add an odd or even number and save.
To use a tape recorder effectively to record information.	Higher and Middle achievers: record a poem you have written on to tape. *The children write their own poems in a literacy session before starting this challenge.* Lower achievers: record a nursery rhyme on to tape.
To use a search engine to find information on a given topic.	Work with a partner to use a search engine to find out something about castles. *The word 'castle' entered in a search engine finds a huge number of entries, including places with castle in their names (Newcastle, Castleford, Barnard Castle, etc.). It's useful to do this first, before discussing with the children how to put additional terms into the engine to narrow the search.*

ICT Challenges Summer 2

Objectives linked to the QCA scheme of work	Challenges
To use a writing programme effectively to write a sentence.	Work in mixed ability pairs. One of the pair is to write a question about a traditional tale. Their partner is to answer it underneath.
To use a word bank to order text on the screen.	Use the given word bank (relating to a traditional tale) and make a sentence.
To develop skills in using the programmable toy.	Higher and Middle achievers: send the pixie to a given location. Make it turn 180 and 360 degrees. Lower achievers: as above but only one turn of 180 degrees.
To use a word bank to order text on the screen. To use a writing programme to add information.	Higher and Middle achievers: use the connectives in the word bank to write 3 sentences about your school day. Save your work. Lower achievers: as above but write only 2 sentences.
To use a tape recorder effectively to record information.	Work in mixed ability pairs. Use a tape recorder to record two classroom sounds. Play it back to your friend and see if they can say what the sounds are.

Geography Challenges Autumn 1

Objectives from NLS	Challenges
Be able to use the correct vocabulary to describe places.	Higher achievers: draw and label your favourite part of the classroom. Middle and lower achievers: draw your favourite part of the classroom and talk to an adult about your picture.
Be able to recognise and name key features in their immediate environment.	Draw an area outside the school. Talk to an adult about which area you have chosen, and why.
Develop their sense of place in relation to their home and school.	Draw at least three landmarks that you see on your way to school (e.g. postbox, shop, bus stop).
Be able to express views on places in their environment.	Draw a special place near your home where you like to go to eat.
Recognise that they have a personal address that differs to those of their peers.	Draw a picture of your home and the people who live there. Remember to write the number on your door.
Be able to compare and contrast two localities.	Write a letter to a character from a story telling them two or three things about yourself and where you live.
Represent in picture form features they would like to see in their local environment.	Draw something that you wish was near to where you live (e.g. park, zoo, shop, cinema).

Geography Challenges Autumn 2

Objectives from NLS	Challenges
Describe a journey they have been on.	Think of a place a long way away that you have been to — maybe somewhere you went on holiday. Draw a picture of it. Write about how you got there.
Be able to identify and name landmarks.	Higher achievers: draw a map with three landmarks, showing how you get from your home to somewhere in the local area (e.g. shops, train station). Other abilities: draw three landmarks that you see on your way from your home to the shops.
Identify the ways in which people who help us contribute to the community.	Draw a picture of what you think a firefighter does to help the community. Write one or two sentences about your picture.
Be able to suggest improvements for safety in the local area.	Draw one or two things that would help to make a busy road safer for pedestrians.
Be able to suggest ways in which we can care for our local environment.	Make a poster encouraging people not to drop litter.
Be able to suggest improvements to the local environment.	Draw a picture of something (or someone) you think we need more of in the area where you live (e.g. buses, policeman/policewoman, litter bins, shops). Write a sentence saying why.

Geography Challenges Spring 2

Objectives from NLS	Challenges
Make observations about different environments.	Compare the place where you live with somewhere you have been on holiday. Write about two or three things that are similar or different.
Be able to recognise different things we do in order to keep clean and healthy.	Draw and label three things that may happen in Calcutta when no rain falls. *Before this challenge the children had spent some time in Geography sessions comparing a locality with which they were familiar (their local area) with another country. They had spent some time talking about India and looking at pictures.*
Understand the importance of keeping ourselves clean and healthy.	Make a poster that identifies three things in Calcutta which help keep people healthy.
Be able to recognise the importance of water.	Make a list of five things which you use water for each day.
Understand that there is a difference between foods we like and those that are important.	Draw and label three foods that are treats and three foods that are necessities.

History Challenges Spring 1

Objectives from NLS	Challenges
Use a range of sources to find out information about toys and games from the past.	Look at the Bruegel picture 'Children's Games'. Draw and describe a game that children may have played a long time ago.
Understand that the design and material can indicate the age of a toy.	Higher and Middle achievers: draw a new and an old toy and describe the differences. Lower achievers: look at the pictures of toys. Divide them into two groups, one group of old and one of new. *This challenge follows a whole class session in which the concepts of old and new are discussed, and related to familiar objects which have been brought to school by the children.*
Describe how their toy choices changes as they get older.	Higher and Middle achievers: draw and label one toy that you played with when you were a baby and one toy that you play with now. Lower achievers: draw and label one toy that you played with when you were a baby.
Find out about toys that belonged to parents/grandparents.	Draw a picture and describe a toy that your grandmother or grandfather may have used. (Children were asked to find out information from their grandparents about toys they used to play with).
Place objects in chronological order using appropriate language.	Higher and Middle achievers: draw three toys on a time line. Label which is the oldest and which is the newest. Lower achievers: draw three toys on a time line.
Identify, describe and label artefacts recognising differences in age and design.	Higher and Middle achievers: make a poster advertising the toy museum. Make sure you tell people what they can see. Lower achievers: make a label for one of the toys in the toy museum.

History Challenges Summer 1

Objectives	Challenges
Understand that people live in different sorts of homes. Recognise common external features of domestic dwellings.	Higher and Middle achievers: draw and label two different homes that you may see near where you live (e.g. flat, semi detached house). Describe two things that are similar and two things that are different about the homes. Lower achievers: draw two different homes that you may see near where you live.
Begin to recognise different homes from the past. Understand how homes have changed over the years.	Higher and Middle achievers: look at the castle on the interactive site. Describe three things about the castle that make it different from your home. Lower achievers: in pairs, look at the castle on the interactive site. Describe one things about the castle that makes it different from your home. *This challenge provides a cross curricular link with the ICT challenge for Summer 1.*
Identify differences between two homes built at different times	Higher and Middle achievers: write three facts comparing a castle (or a Victorian or Edwardian home) with homes you see near to school. *Sources to help children make this comparison include a walk in the local area, discussions, websites, wall posters and books.* Lower achievers: discuss with a partner one fact about a castle(or a Victorian or Edwardian home) that is different from homes you see near to school. Tell a grown-up what you think.
Become familiar with key external aspects of homes from different time periods.	Higher and Middle achievers: make a time line of four homes. *We use pictures of a range of homes – a cave, a castle, a Victorian home and a recently built house.* Lower achievers: cut out and stick the three homes from the past on the time-line, showing the oldest to the newest.

continues over

History Challenges Summer 1 (continued)

Objectives	Challenges
Recognise different rooms and household objects from a long time ago. Describe the characteristics of household objects from a long time ago.	Higher and Middle achievers: sort household objects into old and new. Record and label these in 2 groups in your book. *With the involvement and co-operation of parents, children are encouraged to bring into school a selection of household objects. We build up the collection over several days until we have enough for the challenge.* Lower achievers: cut out the household objects and stick them in your book in two groups, old and new.
Answer questions about household objects used a long time ago. Make inferences about aspects of home life a long time ago.	Higher and Middle achievers: choose four household objects from the past and describe how they might have been used. Lower achievers: as above but only two objects. *The choice is made from the collection of objects used for the challenge above. We talk about the objects as they're brought in, so that children are able to describe their uses.*

Creative Challenges Autumn

Autumn 1	Autumn 2
Draw or make a picture of your own choice.	Draw a firework going off, or make a model of one.
Make a picture using some 2D shapes.	Design and make an artificial light that you could use at night time.
Make a puppet for the 'Three Billy Goats Gruff' story.	Draw a picture or make a decoration for the class Sukkot. *This challenge links with work in RE. A Sukkot is built by Jews as part of their harvest celebrations. It is usually decorated with fruit and colourful pictures.*
Make a basket and present for Little Red Riding Hood's Grandma.	Draw, or make a collage of a character or scene from the Wizard of Oz.
Draw or make a collage of one of the fruits or animals from Handa's Surprise.	Draw, or make a collage of a tasty treat that the Bear may have had in his picnic box. *This challenge relates to the big book currently being used in Literacy sessions – 'This is the Bear and the Picnic Lunch'.*
Make a hat, badge or medal which shows two rhyming words (e.g. a dog on a log, a pig in a wig).	Make a model or picture of a person who helps us in our local area.
Make a colourful invitation to ask the Teddy to a picnic.	Make Christmas decorations for the class grotto.

Creative Challenges Spring

Spring 1	Spring 2
Make a collage of a picture using different textured materials. Describe the materials to your friend.	Draw a picture of something you did or saw in the holidays.
Draw or make a collage picture of one of your own toys using lots of different materials.	Make a 3D sculpture of a minibeast, using things from the junk modelling box.
Draw a picture with an odd and even number of things in it.	Draw, or make a collage of a spider.
Draw or make a collage of your Mum/Dad's Teddy. Think about how you could make it look old.	Design and make a basket for Mother's Day sweets.
Make a puppet for one of the characters from 'Suddenly'.	Draw, or make a collage of one of the animals from an African story. *We use the story 'Handa's Hen', which links with Literacy and Geography work.*
Make a collage of an imaginary character. Give the character a name.	Design and make your own kite. *This is a difficult challenge and requires adult help. The amount and degree of help given depends on the needs of individual children.*

Creative Challenges Summer

Spring 1	Spring 2
Draw a picture which shows some signs of spring, or make a collage.	Design and make a house for the Three Little Pigs.
Draw a picture of an alien or where it may live, or make a collage.	Make a Father's Day card (or a card for someone else special) and write a message inside.
Design and make a colourful flag for a castle.	Design and make an item of clothing in the style of Mary Quant. *Any designer with a distinctive style can be used. In this case an adult providing challenge support shows examples of Mary Quant's designs, which are displayed nearby. The 'making' is usually a paper cut-out, but children who are able to go further are encouraged to do so.*
Choose a Victorian artefact and make a careful picture of it.	Design a poster showing why your school is such a nice place. See how much interesting information you can include.
Create a symmetrical pattern using the different materials.	Make a picture to go on the wall of your new classroom. *This is a free choice activity, and children are able to make any picture they wish in a range of media. Adults are ready to make suggestions if needed.*
Draw or make a collage of your favourite jungle animal.	Make a frame for your picture.

Opportunities for extended free choice writing and numeracy

'Achievement in other areas such as social interaction and confidence, and creativity is also much higher.' (Year One Staff)

'The children, in my opinion, are all doing brilliantly. Their ability and confidence to write is particularly impressive as all the children are always eager to have a go. They are motivated and enthusiastic and seem to genuinely enjoy all their learning.' (Year One Staff)

Higher achiever rewriting the story of Rapunzel during a free choice activity.

Example of lower achiever's word-building during a free choice activity.

'I love the Literacy Challenge the most because I'm getting really good at remembering my finger spaces' (Child)

'I think the children are doing well with their learning. It is a joy to work with children who are willing to have a go at their own spelling because they are confident and know how to sound out.' (Year One Staff)

'My favourite challenge is the Numeracy one. I'm really good at doing sums and sometimes I get the hard ones right.' (Child)

'The children seem really confident about their own abilities in using their number skills.' (Year one Staff)

Higher achiever writing all his numbers to 100 during a free choice activity

Higher achiever, proud of having written all his doubles to 30+30

Lower achiever writing her numbers to 15 during a free choice activity

Opportunities for supporting creativity

'She loves the challenges and I feel it is a positive way of encouraging the children.' (Year One Parent)

'Year 1 is still such a young age and they should be able to explore and experiment informally.' (Year One Staff)

Using collage materials to
make a self portrait

Daddy bear, mummy bear and baby bear

A collage of a lollipop lady, made using
materials from the Creative Area

'I love working on my creative challenge because I can choose different things to use. I like the sparkly paper the best.' (Child)

Opportunities to extend formal learning into play

'Giving the children choices and free time to choose does not mean chaos but gives them a chance to relax, to be creative, to be children and to be in a better frame of mind for more formal learning.' (Year One Staff)

A child building her own house and garden during our 'Local Area' topic.

Children working together to build Noah's Ark after hearing the story as part of RE.

'When I have done my Five Challenges I can choose to do whatever I want. Sometimes I make a picture for my mummy and sometimes I practise my sums on the whiteboard.' (Child)

Opportunities to support sustained thinking

An adult supports some challenges

'The quality of work and the level of involvement is so much higher than before. Also children always finish their work, which didn't happen before, particularly with low achievers.'
(Year One Staff)

'I love doing my challenges. I always try and do five and then I get a treat.'
(Child)

Opportunities for developing peer support and social inclusion

'Peer support is fostered. A lovely example of this was last week when Damien had noticed his friend, Carl (who was a lower achiever) working on his challenge. Damien brought Carl to me and said, "Look at Carl's beautiful work today. He's being a real superstar. Can he have one of your special badges?"!' (Year One Staff)

'Sometimes James gets muddled up with his numbers so I help him sort his answers out.' (Child)

Children supporting one another during a Literacy Challenge

Children helping each other with a Science Challenge, investigating objects that float and sink.

Opportunities for developing social skills across ability groups

'Also achievement in other areas such as social interaction and confidence/creativity is much higher.' (Year One Staff)

Children accessing their own drinks and fruit.

Children working collaboratively to make a kite in the creative area.

'She always comes home with a smile on her face telling me what she has been doing at school.' (Year One Parent)

Continuity & Progression

The books on this page have been produced to help you plan for continuity and progression, from the Foundation Stage and throughout Key Stage 1. They are available direct from Featherstone Education, on our website or from your usual book supplier.

Smooth Transitions

Ensuring continuity from the Foundation Stage

by Ros Bayley & Sally Featherstone

Order STRA   **ISBN 1904187676**

The tensions between the Foundation Stage and KS1 have now been acknowledged. This book offers advice for teachers, teaching assistants, early years practitioners, parents and managers on supporting children through the move from Reception to Year 1. Included is a special section on how we can use new knowledge about how children learn to build on previous learning.

"This is brilliant! I want every infant teacher in Britain to have a copy." Sue Palmer.
"Practical...accessible...invaluable. It will help you do what we all know is right for the children."
Early Years Educator Magazine

> **Several Local Authorities have adopted *Smooth Transitions* as their official guidance on transition to Key Stage 1. We are able to 'personalise' editions by incorporating your own guidance notes, a message or forward and by adding your logo to the cover. Please call to discuss options and prices.**

Many teachers in KS1 are having to cope with children of different ages and stages of development in the same class. These two guides, based on work by teachers in a group of primary schools, show how both the Early Learning Goals and National Curriculum targets can be addressed through the same themes taught across different age groups at the same time.

The two books are different – one offering a two year cycle of themes and the other a three year cycle. Both are also available on CD ROM so that you can easily edit them and adapt them to your own planning. Part of the **Really Good Stuff!** series.

Managing the Curriculum in Mixed Age Classes: Foundation & Y1

Order SG1 (book)   **ISBN 1902233506**
Order SG1D (book+CD ROM)   **ISBN 190223359X**

Managing the Curriculum in Mixed Age Classes: Foundation & KS1

Order SG2 (book)   **ISBN 1902233514**
Order SG2D (book+CD ROM)   **ISBN 1902233603**

Making It Work in Year 1

Order MWY1

ISBN 1905019068

How can the benefits of the Foundation Curriculum be maintained when children move into Key Stage 1? This book suggests ways in which teachers can maintain continuity while ensuring progression in the curriculum, so the needs of all children are met.

Featherstone Education, PO Box 6350, Lutterworth LE17 6ZA

01858 881212   sales@featherstone.uk.com

www.featherstone.uk.com